COMPREHENSIVE ASSURANCE
&
SYSTEMS TOOL

An Integrated Practice Set

FOURTH EDITION

MANUAL MODULE

COMPREHENSIVE ASSURANCE & SYSTEMS TOOL

An Integrated Practice Set

FOURTH EDITION

LAURA R. INGRAHAM

J. GREGORY JENKINS

VIRGINIA POLYTECHNIC INSTITUTE AND STATE UNIVERSITY

MANUAL MODULE

Pearson

New York, NY

Vice President, Business, Economics, and UK Courseware: Donna Battista
Director of Portfolio Management: Adrienne D'Ambrosio
Director, Courseware Portfolio Management: Ashley Dodge
Senior Sponsoring Editor: Neeraj Bhalla
Editorial Assistant: Elisa Marks
Vice President, Product Marketing: Roxanne McCarley
Senior Product Marketer: Tricia Murphy
Product Marketing Assistant: Marianela Silvestri
Manager of Field Marketing, Business Publishing: Adam Goldstein
Executive Field Marketing Manager: Nayke Popovich
Field Marketing Assistant: Jessica Quazza
Vice President, Production and Digital Studio, Arts and Business: Etain O'Dea
Director of Production, Business: Jeff Holcomb
Managing Producer, Business: Melissa Feimer
Content Producer: Sugandh Juneja
Operations Specialist: Carol Melville
Design Lead: Kathryn Foot
Manager, Learning Tools: Brian Surette
Content Developer, Learning Tools: Sarah Peterson
Managing Producer, Digital Studio and GLP, Media Production and Development: Ashley Santora
Managing Producer, Digital Studio and GLP: James Bateman
Managing Producer, Digital Studio: Diane Lombardo
Digital Studio Producer: Mary Kate Murray
Digital Studio Producer: Alana Coles
Digital Content Team Lead: Noel Lotz
Digital Content Project Lead: Martha LaChance
Project Manager: Katherine Tiffany Ragay, SPi Global
Cover Design: Laurie Entringer
Cover Art: Romolo Tavani/Shutterstock
Printer/Binder: LSC Communications, Inc./Harrisonburg
Cover Printer: LSC Communications, Inc./Harrisonburg

Library of Congress Cataloging-in-Publication Data on File

1 18

Pearson

ISBN 10: 0-13-479082-0
ISBN 13: 978-0-13-479082-4

Table of Contents

Preface

The Comprehensive Assurance and Systems Tool (CAST) provides an integrated learning opportunity that encompasses financial statement assurance and accounting information systems issues. CAST uniquely exposes students to these issues at The Winery at Chateau Americana, a hypothetical company that is based on an actual domestic winery. Unlike traditional projects and assignments that may offer little or no context, students develop a rich knowledge and understanding of Chateau Americana and its industry as they provide assurance on the company's financial statements and address a variety of challenging accounting information systems issues.

For students to succeed in the rapidly changing fields of accounting and auditing, they need to think critically and analytically, understand and utilize information technology, and communicate clearly and effectively. We help students develop these skills in CAST in the following ways:

- Each of the modules that underlies CAST—the *Manual AIS module*, the *Computerized Accounting Information Systems module*, and the *Assurance module*—calls on students to apply critical and analytical thinking to understand and resolve problems and challenges related to internal controls, processing and reporting transaction data and financial statements, and the application of auditing standards.

- Students gain valuable hands-on experience in the Manual AIS module and the Computerized Accounting Information Systems module. Using realistic supporting documentation, students record transactions in both a traditional manual accounting system and a computerized accounting system. In addition, students analyze data and build a number of technology-based tools using *Microsoft's Excel* and *Access* and *Sage50*.

- Throughout each of the modules, clear and effective communication are reinforced. Students are called on to develop clear financial statements, explain the factors affecting an audit client's business, and document their performance of common audit procedures.

CAST can be implemented in either an undergraduate or graduate setting and is ideally suited for simultaneous integration across assurance and AIS courses. The Manual Module can also be implemented in an Introductory course. In addition, each of the modules can be completed either as an in-class or an out-of-class assignment. CAST affords students the opportunity to develop and strengthen their analytical thinking, written and oral communication, problem solving, and team building skills.

New to this Edition

The following items are new to the fourth edition of this text:

- Updated instructions and payroll information have been added to the Manual AIS Module.
- The Manual AIS Module contains three all new transaction sets.
- The spreadsheet application in the Computerized AIS Module has been updated to *Excel 2016* and contains additional screen shots and more complete instructions.
- The general ledger package utilized in the Computerized AIS Module has been updated to the 2018 version of *Sage 50 Accounting*.
- The database application in the Computerized AIS Module has been updated to *Access 2016* with provides additional screen shots and instructions.
- All references to the professional auditing standards in the Assurance Module have been revised to reflect the most recently issued standards.
- Industry data and terminology in the Assurance Module have been updated to provide more current information to students in completing the case.

Laura Ingraham
Greg Jenkins

We dedicate this book to our families:
Dan and Casey
Elaine, Anna, Claire and Will

THE MANUAL ACCOUNTING INFORMATION SYSTEM:
The Winery at Chateau Americana

LEARNING OBJECTIVES

After completing and discussing this module, you should be able to:

- Prepare common business documents, accounting transactions and month-end and year-end transactions, including journal entries, journals, and ledgers in order to understand how the accounting cycle operates and to create the financial statements.
- Identify and interpret common control activities designed to capture, summarize, and report business activities.
- Explain the objectives of maintaining an audit trail.
- Identify deficiencies in the design of common business documents.
- Explain the importance of account reconciliations.

BACKGROUND

In this module, you are required to prepare common source documents relating to the various accounting cycles, prepare journal entries, post entries to the general and subsidiary ledgers, prepare trial balances, and prepare a year-end worksheet and the financial statements. While working through this module, you will observe the data flows from their inception to their final reporting.

Due to constraints on students' and instructors' time and resources, the processes outlined in this module focus only on the wholesale segment of the business, picking up after the wine has been manufactured and bottled in the winery and is ready to be sold to distributors.

Company History

Since its founding by Edward Summerfield in 1980, Chateau Americana (CA) has been a small, family-owned winery located in northern California. While CA is comparatively new to the wine industry, it has already cultivated a reputation as one of America's finest wineries. The small, family-owned winery has an impressive vineyard whose 125 acres yields a variety of grapes including Cabernet Sauvignon, Cabernet Franc, Pinot Noir, Chardonnay and Riesling. They have recently purchased more acreage to begin growing additional varieties of their own, specifically Sauvignon Blanc, Merlot and Malbec. CA planted its first grapevines in 1983 and began selling wine in 1988. These vineyards yield approximately 25% of the grapes (or about 800 tons) it requires for wine production. The remaining grapes are purchased from CA's suppliers. In the last several years, CA's wines have received accolades at several highly regarded wine competitions that have dramatically increased the demand for its wines. The company currently has annual sales of 3,850,000 cases.

OVERVIEW OF WINE PRODUCTION

Chateau Americana is a fully operational winery that produces red, white, and sparkling wines.

Red Wine Process

The process for making red wine begins by feeding the grapes into a destemmer/crusher machine. The crushed grapes, skin and seeds, called "must," is then piped into stainless steel fermentation tanks, each of which holds between 3,000 and 5,000 gallons. The must remains in the fermentation tanks at a temperature of 70-75° for a period of 8-21 days and is rotated 4 times a day to break up the skim containing the seeds that float to the surface. The fermentation tank is then emptied. Seventy percent of the juice comes out as "free run," much of which is later used for the more expensive wine labels. The solid remainder is then emptied into a presser that carefully extracts the remaining juice without breaking the seeds.

Red wine is typically aged in oak barrels. Aging of the wine depends upon the number of times the barrel has been used. If the barrel has never been used before, the aging process takes approximately six months. If it has been used once before, the aging process takes approximately 18 months. And if it has been used twice before, the aging process takes approximately 2 years.

White Wine Process

The process of making white wine begins by feeding the white grapes into a bladder press. Inside this machine, a bladder expands, pressing the white grapes between it and the outer shell. Only the juice is then piped into the fermentation tanks where it remains at a temperature of approximately 60° for approximately 30 days while the sugar in the grapes is converted to alcohol.

White wine is most often then aged in stainless steel tanks, although oak barrels may be used.

Bottling

The aged wine is bottled in an atmospherically controlled "clean" room where the air is filtered and exchanged every 60 seconds. Using an automated assembly line, bottles are sterilized, filled, corked, capped, and labeled at a rate of 50 per minute.

OPERATIONS

Organizational Structure and Personnel

CA presently employs 250 permanent employees. Its management team is widely respected in the industry. Because the winery is a family-owned business, the owners have invested considerable time and energies in hiring individuals whom they believe are competent and trustworthy.

Currently, members of the Summerfield family occupy most of the key management positions. Edward Summerfield is the family's patriarch and president of the company. He has received several entrepreneurship awards and is generally perceived as an astute business person. Edward's daughter, Taylor Summerfield, is vice president of marketing for the company. Prior to assuming this position, she had a successful career in sales and marketing. Taylor is well-educated and earned an MBA from an Ivy League school.

Edward's son-in-law, Jacques Dupuis, is vice-president of winery operations. He has an extensive background in viticulture (i.e., grape growing) and vinification (i.e., wine making). Rob Breeden, the company's CFO, is the sole individual to hold a key management position who is not a member of the Summerfield family. He has extensive financial experience and was previously employed in public accounting for nine years and served as controller and CFO for another California winery. Rob holds undergraduate and graduate degrees in accounting and is a CPA.

Chart of Accounts

Chateau Americana has developed a six-digit classification scheme for its Chart of Accounts. The Chart of Accounts is found behind the Year-End Procedures.

CASH SALES INVOICE

Invoice Number **C2228**

Invoice Date 12/3/XX

Chateau Americana, Inc.
3003 Vineyard Way
Huntington, CA 95394
(707) 368-8485
CA-NC-67

Sold To:
Grapevine Selections
2864 Worth Street
Napa, CA 95748

Ship To:
Grapevine Selections
2864 Worth Street
Napa, CA 95748

Salesperson	Customer P.O. Number	Customer Number	ABC Number
RS	7563	0505	P45293X

Product	Description	Size	Quantity	Cost	Extended
W120019	Chenin Blanc	0.750	432	5.25	$ 2,268.00
R130056	Merlot	0.750	324	6.00	1,944.00
R130061	Cabernet Sauvignon	0.750	384	6.50	2,496.00
S140000	Sparkling Brut	0.750	228	11.00	2,508.00

Grand Total Bottles: 1,368

Total Cases: 114

Comments:

Grand Total Cost: $ 9,216.00

Date 12/3/XX
Invoice Number C2228
Customer Number 0505

Distribution: Copy 1 — Accounting; Copy 2 – Shipping; Copy 3 – Customer; Copy 4 – Sales

Figure 1- Sample Invoice

Selling Prices and Costs

Chateau Americana maintains a list of wine costs and selling prices. Wine is sold by the case (12 bottles to a case). The list is found behind the Year-End Procedures.

Date 12/03/XX **Uniform Bill of Lading**

Ship From	**Bill of Lading Number:** 136369
Name: Chateau Americana, Inc. **Address:** 3003 Vineyard Way **City/State/Zip:** Huntington, CA 95394 **SID No.:** 122448	**Carrier Name:** *Pacific Freightliners*
Ship To	**Trailer number:** *ABC 3899*
Name: Grapevine Selections **Address:** 2864 Worth Street **City/State/Zip:** Napa, CA 95748 **CID No.:** 542352	**Serial number(s):** *313734449*
Special Instructions:	**Freight Charge Terms:** (Freight charges are prepaid unless marked otherwise) Prepaid: ☐ Collect: ☒ 3rd Party: ☐ ☐ **(check box):** Master bill of lading with attached underlying bills of lading.

Customer Order Information

Description of Items	Quantity	Weight	Pallet/Slip (circle one)		Additional Shipper Information
Wine	*114*	*3,876*	(Y)	N	
			Y	N	
			Y	N	
			Y	N	
Grand Total					

Where the rate is dependent on value, shippers are required to state specifically in writing the agreed or declared value of the property as follows: "The agreed or declared value of the property is specifically stated by the shipper to be not exceeding ____________ per ____________."	**COD Amount:** $ 9,216.00 **Free terms:** ☐ Collect ☐ Prepaid ☒ Customer check acceptable

Note: Liability limitation for loss or damage in this shipment may be applicable. See 49 USC §14706(c)(1)(A) & (B)

Received, subject to individually determined rates or contracts that have been agreed upon in writing between the carrier and shipper, if applicable, otherwise to the rates, classifications and rules that have been established by the carrier and are available to the shipper, on request, and to all applicable state and federal regulations.	**The carrier shall not make delivery of this shipment without payment of and all other lawful charges.** **Shipper Signature** *Jerry Richards*

Shipper Signature/Date This is to certify that the above named materials are properly classified, packaged, marked and labeled, and are in proper condition for transportation according to the applicable regulations of the DOT. *Jerry Richards* *12/03/XX*	**Trailer Loaded:** ☐ By shipper ☒ By driver	**Carrier Signature/Pickup Date** Carrier acknowledges receipt of packages and required placards. Carrier certifies emergency response information was made available and/or carrier has the DOT emergency response guidebook or equivalent documentation in the vehicle. **Property described above is received in good order, except as noted.** *Bruce Garrett* *12/03/XX*

Distribution: Copy 1 — Accounting; Copy 2 – Shipping; Copy 3 – Customer

Figure 2 – Sample Bill of Lading

Processes

Sales. Chateau Americana sells its wine to most distributors on account and offers a few select distributors credit terms as detailed below. Sales to a small number of distributors are cash sales. When a purchase order is received from a distributor, a sales invoice (*Figure 1*) is generated and the requested items are pulled from finished goods inventory. Copies 1, 2 and 3 of the Invoice are sent to Shipping where the Bill of Lading (*Figure 2*) is prepared in triplicate. Copy 3 of the Bill of Lading and Copy 3 of the Invoice are sent to the Customer with the wine. Copy 2 of the Bill of Lading and Copy 2 of the Invoice are filed numerically by the Shipping department. Copy 1 of the Bill of Lading and Copy 1 of the Invoice are sent to Accounting where the Accounting Clerk updates the Sales Register. Copy 1 of the Bill of Lading and Copy 1 of the Invoice are then filed numerically.

The Sales Register is totaled monthly and then posted to the General Ledger.

Credit Memo

Chateau Americana, Inc.
3003 Vineyard Way
Huntington, CA 95394

Phone: (707)368-8485

Credit Memo : 2753	
Date: 1/8/XX	**Salesperson:** CEZ
Customer Number: 2201	**Customer PO No:** 10654
Amount Net: $267.00	

Credit To: *Veritas Distributors Inc*

Comments:

Returned damaged cases of wine

Item # / Description	Quantity	Price: Unit Price	Price: Amount
R130061 / Cabernet Sauvignon	12	$6.50	$78.00
W120019 / Chenin Blanc	36	$5.25	$189.00

Customer Name: *Veritas Distributors Inc*

Credit: Amount:: $267.00

Chateau Americana, Inc.
3003 Vineyard Way
Huntington, CA 95394
Phone: (707)368-8485

Credit Date: 1/8/XX

Credit Memo #: **2753**

Customer Number: 2201

Distribution: Copy 1 – Accounting; Copy 2 – Customer

Figure 3 – Sample Credit Memo

Sales Tax. Sales tax is not assessed on wholesale sales. Therefore, there is no sales tax applied to sales to distributors.

Credit Terms. Chateau Americana offers discounts for early payment to certain select distributors who have done business with CA for an extended period. The terms offered to these distributors are 3/15, net 30. Most other distributors are granted credit terms without early payment discounts.

Returns and Allowances. Credit memos (*Figure 3*) are issued for price corrections, overshipments, or when a shipment has been damaged in transit. Due to legal restrictions, wine cannot be returned to regular inventory. On the very rare occasions that wine is returned, it is put into special inventory for taxed wines.

Purchase Order

Bill to

Chateau Americana, Inc.
3003 Vineyard Way
Huntington, CA 95394

Phone:(707)368-8485
Supplier No.: P1892

PO #: 9682

Date: 3/20/XX **Date Required:** 3/28/XX

Terms: Net 30
Shipped: Longhorn Shippers, Inc.
Buyer: Franz Bieler

Supplier
Crown Packaging, Inc.
1102 Commerce Street
Dallas. TX 75391

Phone: (214)555-1212

Ship To
Chateau Americana
3003 Vineyard Way
Huntington, CA 95394

Item #	Description	Size	Quantity	Unit Price	Amount
CAPCE12	Crème Caps Wine		2318	$ 0.110	$ 254.98
CAPGD12	Gold Caps Wine		2404	0.089	213.96
CAPGN12	Green Caps Wine		31173	0.095	2,961.44
CAPRD12	Red Caps Wine		7527	0.100	752.70
				Total Amount	$ 4,183.08
				Tax	
				Total Invoice	$ 4,183.08

Message

Authorization

Name:	Michelle Radcliff
Date:	3/23/XX
Title:	Purchasing Supervisor
Signature:	*Michelle Radcliff*

Distribution: Copy 1 — Supplier; Copy 2 – Accounting; Copy 3 – Receiving; Copy 4 – Purchasing

Figure 4 – Sample Purchase Order

Cash Receipts. The mail is received by the receptionist who opens it in the presence of another individual. At that time, all checks are restrictively endorsed by the receptionist. She also prepares and signs a cash receipts summary. The receptionist then prepares and takes a deposit slip, along with the checks, to the bank for deposit on a daily basis. The validated deposit slip received from the bank, remittance advices from the checks, and cash receipts summary are sent to accounting.

After receiving the validated deposit slip, remittance advices from the checks, and the cash receipts summary, the Accounting Clerk inputs the transactions, updates the cash receipts journal, and the accounts receivable subsidiary ledger if the cash received was from a credit customer. The validated deposit slip, cash receipts summary, and remittance advices are filed together chronologically. The cash receipts journal is totaled monthly and posted to the general ledger.

The Accounting Clerk prepares monthly customer statements in duplicate. Copy 2 is filed alphabetically in Accounting. Copy 1 is mailed to the customer.

Receiving Report

Date Received: *3/28/XX*
Receiving Report #: **14891**

Received from *Crown Packaging, Inc.*
Purchase Order # *9682*

Freight carrier *Longhorn Shippers, Inc.*
Received by *BH*

Quantity	Item #	Size	Description
2318	*CAPCE12*		*Crème Cabs Wine*
2404	*CAPGD12*		*Gold Cabs Wine*
31173	*CAPGN12*		*Green Cabs Wine*
7527	*CAPRD12*		*Red Cabs Wine*

Condition:

Excellent

Distribution: Copy 1 — Accounting; Copy 2 – Purchasing; Copy 3 – Receiving

Figure 5 – Sample Receiving Report

Purchases. As raw materials are needed for production and bottling, a prenumbered purchase order is completed (*Figure 4*) in quadruplicate. The purchase order must be approved and signed by a purchasing supervisor. Copy 1 of the purchase order is sent to the supplier. Copy 2 of the purchase order is sent to Accounting. Copy 3 of the purchase order is sent to Receiving. Copy 4 of the purchase order and the purchase requisition are held temporarily in Purchasing. As goods are received from suppliers, they are inspected, counted and compared to copy 3 of the purchase order. A prenumbered receiving report is prepared in triplicate (*Figure 5*). Copy 3 of the receiving report and copy 3 of the purchase order are filed numerically. Copy 2 of the receiving report is sent to Purchasing where it is matched with copy 4 of the purchase order and the purchase requisition and filed numerically. Copy 1 is sent to Accounting where it is matched with Copy 2 of the purchase order.

Cash Disbursements. When invoices are received for items or services not requiring a receiving report or a purchase order, they are first routed to the appropriate department for approval (by the receptionist when she opens the mail). The approved invoice is then sent to Accounting.

When invoices for inventory are received from suppliers, the receptionist sends them directly to Accounting. These invoices are matched with copy 1 of the receiving report and copy 2 of the purchase order. They are then entered into the purchases journal. The purchases journal is totaled monthly and then posted to the general ledger.

Supplier invoices, copy 1 of the receiving report, and copy 2 of the purchase order are then filed in a temporary file by due date to insure that they will be paid on a timely basis and that any discounts offered will be taken. Supplier invoices not requiring receiving reports and/or purchase orders are also included in this temporary file. As the invoices come due, the accounting clerk pulls them from the temporary file and writes the checks. The accounting supervisor reviews the supporting documentation such as the check, invoice, copy 1 of the receiving report, and copy 2 of the purchase order for completeness, initials the invoices, and sends the documentation (commonly referred to as a voucher package) to the chief financial officer (CFO) for signature.

The CFO reviews the package for reasonableness, signs the checks, stamps the documents "Paid," and returns the package to Accounting. The checks are then mailed. The remaining documents are filed numerically by check number.

The cash disbursements journal is totaled monthly and posted to the general ledger.

Inventory. Chateau Americana maintains a perpetual inventory system for both production inventory and for finished goods (bottled wines). The perpetual inventory records are updated based on the standard cost buildups for each bottled wine when inventory is moved from the bottling room to the warehouse. (Again, you are reminded that this module focuses only on the wholesale segment of the business and does not deal with production or selling of basic grape-stock).

A physical inventory is taken at the end of the year for production inventory and at the end of each quarter for finished goods inventory. Adjusting entries are made as necessary based on the physical inventory counts.

Payroll. Chateau Americana pays its employees on the 15th and the last day of each month. The department supervisors are responsible for approving and initialing the time cards for any hourly employees in their respective departments. The time cards are then sent to Accounting at the end of the payroll period. The accounting clerk calculates payroll for each employee using the current payroll information found in the employee payroll subsidiary ledgers. The accounting clerk enters the payroll into the payroll journal and posts to the employee payroll subsidiary ledgers. The time cards are then filed chronologically and alphabetically.

The accounting clerk prepares the payroll checks from the payroll checking account based upon the information from the payroll journal and enters the check number in the payroll journal. The accounting clerk also prepares a check drawn from the general checking account payable to the payroll checking account in the amount of the total payroll to cover the current period's payroll. The accounting supervisor reviews the payroll check and the check from the general checking account and initials the payroll journal before forwarding all the checks to the CFO for signature. The CFO reviews and signs the checks and returns them to Accounting. Accounting distributes the payroll checks to the employees and deposits the check for the payroll checking account in the bank.

For payroll purposes, you will be preparing the payroll for four employees: two members of middle management who are salaried employees (Anna Johnson and José Rodriguez) and two production workers who are hourly employees (Tom Bryan and Bob Hissom).

Anna Johnson is an Accounting Supervisor and has been with Chateau Americana for two years. José Rodriguez is a Shift Supervisor and has been with the company for 10 years. Both Bryan and Hissom are in the Operations Department. Bryan is a shift worker in the Wine Presses, and Hissom is a receiving clerk. Both have been with the company for several years.

Employees are paid for holidays. Hourly employees who work more than eight hours in one day receive overtime pay. Overtime hours are paid at a rate of 150% of the regular hourly pay per overtime hour worked.

The amount of federal income tax withheld for each employee is determined (a) by taking into account the employee's marital status and the number of withholding allowances claimed by the employee (both of which can be found in the employee payroll subsidiary ledgers) and (b) referring to the percentage method of withholding of IRS Publication 15. (**HINT:** You can find IRS Publication 15, also entitled "Circular E, Employer's Tax Guide, on the Internet.) You will also need to calculate FICA & Medicare withholdings.

NOTE: For simplification purposes, state withholdings are not calculated in this exercise. The employee FICA withholding rate is 6.2%, while the Medicare rate is 1.45%. These rates will be used to calculate payroll in this text.

Fixed Assets. Depreciation expense is calculated monthly. All assets are depreciated on the straight-line basis using the half-year convention in the year of purchase and the year of sale. A portion of the Fixed Asset subsidiary ledgers has been reproduced for you. Date of acquisition, estimated useful life, acquisition value, and accumulated depreciation for each asset are listed in the ledgers.

TRANSACTION SET A

The books have been posted through December 15, 20XX. The following selected transactions have been extracted from the period December 16 through December 31, 20XX and are to be completed in accordance with the policies and procedures explained above. Documents to be completed can be found in the Document Packet. For all required signatures on these documents sign your name. Supporting documentation for the transactions is provided behind the Year-End Procedures followed by all necessary journals and ledgers.

Note that the current year transactions are denoted as 20XX; prior year transactions are denoted as 20XW; transactions for the subsequent year are denoted as 20XY. Your instructor will provide you with the appropriate current year and you can fill in the dates accordingly for all transactions.

December	Transaction
16	Receive a purchase order from California Premium Beverage (page 17). Fill and ship the order. Complete Invoice No. 15535, Bill of Lading No. 136480 and record the sale in the journals and ledgers. W. A. Bierkstahler is the sales account representative. Relevant data: shipment weight - 12,532 lbs., trailer # - 122302, serial # - 999356278. The carrier is CA Express. Leave the CID No. blank.
16	Order 32 tons of white grapes at $1,875.00 per ton from Mendocino Vineyards. The item number for the white grapes is WG1003. Complete Purchase Order No. 9682. Relevant data: date required - Dec. 22, shipper - Longhorn Shippers, Inc., buyer - Franz Bieler, supplier # - M0652.
16	Purchase a 20XW Ford truck for $26,540.00. The terms include a $4,540.00 down payment and a 3-year, 6% promissory note to Ford Credit for the remaining $22,000.00. Principal and interest on the note are due monthly beginning January 4, 20XY. The company expects the truck to have a useful life of 5 years and no salvage value. Prepare Check No. 19257 payable to Potter Valley Ford for the down payment and record the transaction in the journals and ledgers.
16	The Board of Directors of Chateau Americana authorized a $50,000 cash dividend payable on January 20th to the stockholders of record on January 15th.
17	Receive a phone complaint from Seaside Distributors about a case of Chenin Blanc that was damaged in shipment. The case was part of Invoice No. 15175, dated November 5, 20XX, in the amount of $20,438.40. Seaside paid the invoice on November 19, 20XX and took advantage of the discount (terms 3/15, net 30). Prepare Credit Memo No. 2753 to write-off the damaged inventory that was not returned, and prepare Check No. 19286 to reimburse Seaside for the damaged goods. Record the transactions in the journals and ledgers. W. A. Bierkstahler is the sales account representative. Relevant data: customer PO # - MZ5713. (Note: Be sure to review ***Returns and Allowances*** on Page 6.)

December	Transaction
19	Receive $850 refund from California Wine & Cheese Monthly for overpayment of advertising costs (page 18). Enter the receipt on Cash Receipts Summary No. 5712 and record the cash receipt in the journals and ledgers.
19	Receive payment in full from Pacific Distribution Co. on Invoice No. 15243 dated November 13, 20XX, in the amount of $19,576.80 (page 19). Enter the receipt on Cash Receipts Summary No. 5712 and record the cash receipt in the journals and ledgers.
19	Receive a purchase order (page 20) with payment (page 21) from Sonoma Distributors. Fill and ship the order. Complete Invoice No. C2489, enter the receipt on Cash Receipts Summary No. 5712, and record the sale in the journals and ledgers. W. A. Bierkstahler is the sales account representative. Relevant data: shipment weight - 7,650 lbs., trailer # - 279AJ1, serial # - 919515094. (Hint: Use the Other Account column to post Inventory and Cost of Goods Sold.) **DO NOT** create a Bill of Lading for this purchase order.
22	Receive 19 tons of cabernet sauvignon grapes at $2,279.00 per ton from Mendocino Vineyards. Also received Invoice No. M7634 from Mendocino Vineyards with the shipment (page 22). Terms on the invoice are 2/10, net 30. Complete Receiving Report No. 17251 and record the inventory in the journals and ledgers using the gross method.
26	Receive utility bill from Pacific Gas and Electric in the amount of $18,887.62 (page 23). Prepare Check No. 19402 and record the payment in the journals and ledgers.
30	Receive Brokerage Advice from Edwards Jones for purchase of 500 shares of Microsoft at $65.73 per share plus $400 broker's commission (page 24). Prepare Check No. 19468 and record the purchase in the journals and ledgers.
30	Prepare Check No. 19473 payable to Mendocino Vineyards for the shipment received on December 22 and record the payment in the journals and ledgers.
31	Receive payment in full for the December 16 purchase from California Premium Beverage (page 25). Enter the cash receipt on Cash Receipts Summary No. 5718 and record the cash receipt in the journals and ledgers.
31	Prepare Payroll Checks (Nos. 7111-7114) for Anna Johnson, José Rodriguez, Tom Bryan, and Bob Hissom. Time cards for Tom and Bob are on pages 26-27. Prepare Check No. 19474 to transfer cash from the general cash account to the payroll account. Record the payroll transactions and all appropriate *accruals* in the journals and ledgers.
31	Prepare Check No. 19475 to repay $50,000 of the principal on long-term debt to Bank of Huntington and record the payment in the journals and ledgers.

MONTH-END PROCEDURES

1. **Calculate monthly accrued interest expense for the installment note to Ford Credit (based on 365 days per year and interest starting to accrue on December 17, 20XX). Make the appropriate adjusting entry. The payable is posted to Other Accrued Expenses Payable.**

2. **For your convenience, depreciation in the amount of $105,341.50 has been calculated on all assets for the month of December except for any current purchases of assets. Calculate the depreciation for the Ford Pickup purchased on December 16. Post the depreciation to the Fixed Asset Subsidiary Ledger and add the amount of depreciation expense to the rest of the December depreciation. Make the appropriate adjusting entry.**

3. **The accounting clerk receives the bank statement on a monthly basis and reconciles it to the cash receipts and cash disbursements journals, identifying the necessary adjusting journal entries such as bank services charges, etc. The bank statement for the General Checking Account (Account #111000) reports a balance of $_______ as of December 31, 20XX. (NOTE: You will need to obtain the bank statement balance for the current year from your instructor.) The accounting clerk notes that there are outstanding checks totaling $88,097.31 (checks 19469, 19470, and 19471) and deposits in transit of $41,261.47. In addition, the bank statement indicates bank charges of $30, a returned check from Alota Wine Distributors in the amount of $19,475.26, and a check printing fee of $60. Reconcile the cash balance for the General Checking Account.**

4. **Foot and cross foot the journals & registers. Post all monthly totals from the journals/registers to the General Ledger and post the individual entries in the General Journal to the General Ledger.**

5. **Reconcile the Accounts Receivable Subsidiary Ledger, Accounts Payable Subsidiary Ledger and the Perpetual Inventory Subsidiary Ledger to the General Ledger.**

YEAR-END PROCEDURES

1. **Prepare the unadjusted trial balance using the electronic year-end worksheet provided to you on the CAST web site (your instructor will provide you with the URL for this web site).**

2. **Foot and cross foot the Payroll Subsidiary Ledgers.**

3. **Prepare the year-end adjusting journal entries:**

   a. **Calculate the allowance for bad debts using the net sales method. Experience indicates that 0.05% of net sales should be set aside for bad debts. Make the appropriate adjusting entry.**

   b. **The calculation of federal income tax expense is a year-end adjusting entry but it cannot be made until all other entries have been made and net income before taxes has been determined. Therefore, you**

must first complete the year-end worksheet and calculate net income before taxes. Then calculate federal income tax expense and post the adjusting entry to the worksheet. (HINT: Use rates in effect as of January 20XX. You can find these rates in any tax textbook or by referring to the instructions for Schedule J, Form 1120.)

4. **Complete the remainder of the electronic year-end worksheet.**
5. **Prepare the financial statements including the income statement, the statement of retained earnings, balance sheet, and the statement of cash flows (using the indirect method).**
6. **Prepare and record the closing journal entries in the journal and general ledger.**
7. **Prepare the electronic post-closing trial balance worksheet.**

The Winery at Chateau Americana
Chart of Accounts

Assets (100000)		
Cash (110000)		
	General Checking Account	111000
	Payroll Checking Account	112000
	Money Market Account	113000
	Savings Account	114000
	Petty Cash	119000
Accounts Receivable (120000)		
	Accounts Receivable	121000
	Allowance for Bad Debts	129000
Inventory (140000)		
	Inventory – Production	141000
	Inventory – Finished Goods	145000
Prepaid Expenses		150000
Land and Buildings		160000
Equipment		170000
Accumulated Depreciation		180000
Investments		191000
Liabilities (200000)		
Accounts Payable		210000
Accrued Expenses (220000)		
	Federal Income Tax Withheld	222100
	FICA Withheld	222200
	Medicare Withheld	222300
Payroll Taxes Payable (223000)		
	FICA Payable – Employer	223100
	Medicare Payable – Employer	223200
	Unemployment Taxes Payable	223300
Other Accrued Expenses		230000
	Federal Income Taxes Payable	235000
	Property Taxes Payable	236000
	Dividends Payable	239000
Mortgages Payable		240000
Other Long-Term Payables (260000)		
	Notes Payable	261000
Owners' Equity (300000)		
Common Stock		310000
Paid-in Capital in Excess of Par – Common		311000
Dividends – Common		312000
Retained Earnings		390000
Income (400000)		
	Sales	410000
	Sales Discounts	420000
	Sales Returns and Allowances	430000
	Gain/Loss – Fixed Assets	451000

	Gain/Loss – Marketable Securities	452000
	Dividend Income	491000
	Interest Income	492000
Cost of Goods Sold		510000
Expenses (600000 – 700000)		
Payroll Expense (600000)		
	Wages and Salaries Expense	601000
	Sales Commission Expense	601500
	FICA Tax Expense	602100
	Medicare Tax Expense	602200
	FUTA Expense	602300
	SUTA Expense	602400
Occupancy Expense (610000)		
	Utilities Expense	611000
	Irrigation & Waste Disposal Expense	611300
	Landscaping Expense	612000
Marketing (620000)		
	Advertising Expense	621000
	Marketing Expense	623000
	Festivals & Competitions Expense	624000
Communications Expense (630000)		
	Telephone Expense	631000
	Internet & Computer Expense	632000
	Postage Expense	633000
Professional Services Expense (640000)		
	Legal & Accounting Fees	641000
	Other Consulting Fees	643000
Supplies Expense (650000)		
	Office Supplies Expense	651000
Data Processing Expense		660000
Depreciation Expense		670000
Travel and Entertainment Expense		680000
Insurance Expense (690000)		
	Other Insurance	691000
	Medical Insurance	692000
	Workmen's Compensation Insurance	693000
	Other Employee Benefits Expense	699000
Dues and Subscriptions Expense		700000
Tax Expense (710000)		
	Federal Income Tax Expense	711000
	Property Tax Expense	712000
Maintenance Expense (720000)		
	Repairs and Maintenance Expense	721000
Automobile Expense		731000
Lease Expense		740000
Other Operating Expense (790000)		
	Bad Debt Expense	791000
	Miscellaneous Expense	792000
	Interest Expense	793000

The Winery at Chateau Americana
Price List

Inventory Code	Description	Standard Cost (per bottle)	Selling Price (per bottle)
R130064	Cabernet Franc	$ 5.17	$ 10.91
R130061	Cabernet Sauvignon	5.00	9.55
R130056	Merlot	5.00	9.75
R130072	Shiraz	5.15	11.25
W120080	Chardonnay	9.58	13.15
W120019	Chenin Blanc	4.75	8.98
W120015	Riesling	5.55	9.85
W120016	Sauvignon Blanc	5.60	10.50
S140000	Sparkling Brut	10.52	15.99

PURCHASE ORDER

California Premium Beverage

39848 South Street
Santa Rosa, CA 95402
Phone (707) 555-7451 Fax (707) 555-7452

To:
Chateau Americana
3003 Vineyard Way
Huntington, CA 95394

Ship To:
California Premium Beverage
39848 South Street
Santa Rosa, CA 95402

ABC Permit #: A59782

P.O. DATE	P.O. NUMBER	SHIPPED VIA	F.O.B. POINT	TERMS
12/13/XX	8746	CA Express	Destination	3/15, net 30

ITEM NO	QTY	SIZE	DESCRIPTION	UNIT PRICE	TOTAL
W120015	1512	0.750	Riesling	9.85	14,893.20
W120016	504	0.750	Sauvignon Blanc	10.50	5,292.00
W120019	336	0.750	Chenin Blanc	8.98	3,017.28
R130061	1176	0.750	Cabernet Sauvignon	9.55	11,230.80
R130056	672	0.750	Merlot	9.75	6,552.00
S140000	240	0.750	Sparkling Brut	15.99	3,837.60
W120080	336	0.750	Chardonnay	13.15	4,418.40
				TOTAL	49,241.28

Jorge Gonzalez — Authorized by
12/13/XX — Date

California Wine and Cheese Monthly **23545**
573 Parkins Ave.
Ukiah, CA 95482

Lone Star Bank
Dallas, TX 27540

Date 12/15/XX

PAY Eight Hundred Fifty and 00/100 Dollars -- $ 850.00

To the order of
Chateau Americana
3003 Vineyard Way
Huntington, CA 95394

- SAMPLE, DO NOT CASH -

⑆000000⑆: ⑈000000000⑈ 23545

California Wine and Cheese Monthly **23545**

Reference	Amount
Overpayment of monthly advertising	$850.00

Pacific Distribution Company
10034 Westborough Boulevard
San Francisco, CA 94080

Bank of America
San Francisco, CA 94104

69712

Date 12/16/XX

PAY Nineteen Thousand Five Hundred Seventy Six and 80/100 Dollars ------------------ $ 19,576.80

To The Order Of
Chateau Americana
3003 Vineyard Way
Huntington, CA 95394

- SAMPLE, DO NOT CASH -

⑆:000000⑆: :000000000: 69712

Pacific Distribution Company **69712**

Reference	Net Amount
Invoice #15243, customer # 0505	$19,576.80

PURCHASE ORDER

PO Number: 4376
Date: 12/19/XX

To:
Chateau Americana
3003 Vineyard Way
Huntington, CA 95394

Ship To:
SONOMA DISTRIBUTORS
3224 Greenlawn Street
Ukiah, CA 95482
Phone (707) 555-1705 Fax (707) 555-1706

SHIPPED VIA	ABC #	F.O.B. POINT	TERMS
United Express	A557912	Huntington	Cash

ITEM NO	QTY	SIZE	DESCRIPTION	UNIT PRICE	TOTAL
W120015	480	0.750	Riesling	9.85	4,728.00
W120080	468	0.750	Chardonnay	13.15	6,154.20
W120019	300	0.750	Chenin Blanc	8.98	2,694.00
R130072	780	0.750	Shiraz	11.25	8,775.00
R130056	672	0.750	Merlot	9.75	6,552.00
				TOTAL	28,903.20

Chrystal Harrington 12/19/XX
Authorized by Date

Sonoma Distributors
3224 Greenlawn Street
Ukiah, CA 95482

Humboldt Bank
Ukiah, CA 95482

17003

Date 12/19/XX

PAY Twenty-eight Thousand Nine Hundred Three and 20/100 Dollars --------------- $ 28,903.20

To the order of Chateau Americana
3003 Vineyard Way
Huntington, CA 95394

- SAMPLE, DO NOT CASH -

¦:000000¦: :000000000: 17003

Sonoma Distributors **17003**

Reference	Discount	Net Amount
Payment for PO 4376		$28,903.20

CUSTOMER INVOICE

Invoice Number **M7634**

Invoice Date 12/20/20XX

Mendocino Vineyards
8654 Witherspoon Way
Hopland, CA 95449
Phone: (707) 555-1890

Sold To:
Chateau Americana, Inc.
3003 Vineyard Way
Huntington, CA 95394

Credit Terms: 2/10, Net 30

Ship To:
Chateau Americana, Inc.
3003 Vineyard Way
Huntington, CA 95394

Customer I.D	Customer P.O. Number
CHATAM	9660

Description	Product Number	Quantity	Cost	Extended
Cabernet Sauvignon Grapes	CS1250	19 tons	$2,279.00	$43,301.00

Total Cost: $43,301.00

Comments:

Distribution: Copy 1 — Accounting; Copy 2 – Shipping; Copy 3 – Customer

Payment Coupon

Bill Date: 12/23/20XX

Please Pay by 01/17/20XX
$18,887.62

Amount Enclosed

Account No. 21790-1879

Chateau Americana, Inc.
3003 Vineyard Way
Huntington, CA 95394

Send Payment to:

Pacific Gas and Electric
P.O. Box 2575
San Francisco, CA 94103

Retain bottom portion for your records, detach and return stub with payment.

Service	Chateau Americana, Inc.	Your Account Number	Rate Class	Billing Date
For:	3003 Vineyard Way Huntington, CA 95394	**21790-1879**	**Commercial**	**12/23/20XX**

Meter Number	Service Period	Days	Type of Reading	Multiplier	Units	Meter Readings Current	Meter Readings Past	Usage
68869800	**11/23/XX – 12/23/XX**	**31**	**Actual**	**1**	**KWH**	**1098412**	**1001301**	**97111**
Previous Balance								16,895.53
Payment								16,895.53
Balance Forward								0.00
Current Charges								18,887.62
							Due Date 01/17/20XX	**Total Due** 18,887.62

Pacific Gas and Electric
1000 Energy Drive, San Francisco, CA 94103, (415) 973-8943

Edward Jones Financial Services

100 Market Street
San Francisco, CA 94109
(415)504-9000

Customer
Chateau Americana, Inc.
3003 Vineyard Way
Huntington, CA 95394

Account Number
02334-85763

Tax Identification #
23-7788954

SAVE THIS STATEMENT FOR TAX PURPOSES

Date	Description	Symbol	Fees and/or Commissions($)	Net Dollar Amount ($)	Share Price ($)	Transaction Shares
12/30/03	Microsoft Corporation Common Shares	MSFT	400.00	32,865.00	65.73	500.0000

California Premium Beverage
39848 South Street
Santa Rosa, CA 95402

Bay View Bank
Santa Rosa, CA 95407

21803

Date 12/29/XX

PAY Forty-Seven Thousand Seven Hundred Sixty-Four and 04/100 Dollars ----------------- $ 47,764.04

To The Order Of
Chateau Americana
3003 Vineyard Way
Huntington, CA 95394

- SAMPLE, DO NOT CASH -

⑆000000⑆ ⑈000000000⑈ 21803

California Premium Beverage **21803**

Reference	Discount	Net Amount
# 0504 Invoice 15535	$1,477.24	$47,764.04

Period Ending			December 19, 20XX
Employee Name			Thomas P. Bryan
Signature			*Tom Bryan*
Approved			*PJB*
Out		7th Day	
In			
Out			
In			
Out	4	6th Day	04:00 PM
In			12:01 PM
Out	4		11:30 AM
In			07:29 AM
Out	4	5th Day	04:01 PM
In			12:00 PM
Out	4		11:30 AM
In			07:31 AM
Out	4	4th Day	04:02 PM
In			11:58 AM
Out	4		11:30 AM
In			07:30 AM
Out	4	3rd Day	04:03 PM
In			11:59 AM
Out	4		11:30 AM
In			07:31 AM
Out		2nd Day	
In			
Out			
In			
Out		1st Day	
In			
Out			
In			

Period Ending			December 26, 20XX
Employee Name			Thomas P. Bryan
Signature			*Tom Bryan*
Approved			*PJB*
Out		7th Day	
In			
Out			
In			
Out	4	6th Day	
In			
Out	4		
In			*Holiday*
Out	4	5th Day	
In			
Out	4		
In			*Holiday*
Out	4	4th Day	04:00 PM
In			12:02 PM
Out	4		11:30 AM
In			07:29 AM
Out	4	3rd Day	04:00 PM
In			12:01 PM
Out	4		11:33 AM
In			07:30 AM
Out	4	2nd Day	04:04 PM
In			12:02 PM
Out	4		11:31 AM
In			07:28 AM
Out		1st Day	
In			
Out			
In			

Period Ending			December 31, 20XX
Employee Name			Thomas P. Bryan
Signature			*Tom Bryan*
Approved			*PJB*
Out		7th Day	
In			
Out			
In			
Out		6th Day	
In			
Out			
In			
Out		5th Day	
In			
Out			
In			
Out	4	4th Day	04:02 PM
In			11:58 AM
Out	4.75		11:30 AM
In			06:45 AM
Out	4.5	3rd Day	04:33 PM
In			11:59 AM
Out	4		11:30 AM
In			07:31 AM
Out	5	2nd Day	05:00 PM
In			12:01 PM
Out	4		11:30 AM
In			07:29 AM
Out		1st Day	
In			
Out			
In			

Period Ending	December 19, 20XX		
Employee Name	Robert T. Hissom		
Signature	*Bob Hissom*		
Approved	*PJB*		
Out		7th Day	
In			
Out			
In			
Out	4	6th Day	04:02 PM
In			12:01 PM
Out	4		11:30 AM
In			07:29 AM
Out	4	5th Day	03:59 PM
In			12:02 PM
Out	4		11:30 AM
In			07:27 AM
Out	4	4th Day	04:00 PM
In			11:59 AM
Out	4		11:30 AM
In			07:31 AM
Out	4	3rd Day	04:03 PM
In			12:02PM
Out	4		11:34 AM
In			07:30 AM
Out		2nd Day	
In			
Out			
In			
Out		1st Day	
In			
Out			
In			

Period Ending	December 26, 20XX		
Employee Name	Robert T. Hissom		
Signature	*Bob Hissom*		
Approved	*PJB*		
Out		7th Day	
In			
Out			
In			
Out	4	6th Day	
In			
Out	4		
In			*Holiday*
Out	4	5th Day	
In			
Out	4		
In			*Holiday*
Out	4	4th Day	04:03 PM
In			12:04 PM
Out	4		11:30 AM
In			07:29 AM
Out	4	3rd Day	04:00 PM
In			12:00 PM
Out	4		11:33 AM
In			07:30 AM
Out	4	2nd Day	04:03 PM
In			12:01 PM
Out	4		11:31 AM
In			07:31 AM
Out		1st Day	
In			
Out			
In			

Period Ending	December 31, 20XX		
Employee Name	Robert T. Hissom		
Signature	*Bob Hissom*		
Approved	*PJB*		
Out		7th Day	
In			
Out			
In			
Out		6th Day	
In			
Out			
In			
Out		5th Day	
In			
Out			
In			
Out	4	4th Day	04:00 PM
In			11:58 AM
Out	4		11:32 AM
In			07:32 AM
Out	4	3rd Day	04:01 PM
In			11:59 AM
Out	4		11:30 AM
In			07:30 AM
Out	4	2nd Day	03:57PM
In			11:55 AM
Out	4		11:30 AM
In			07:26 AM
Out		1st Day	
In			
Out			
In			

GENERAL JOURNAL

Date	GL Acct #	Explanation	Post Ref*	Debit	Credit

***Note: Posting reference is "GL and Page Number." For example, GL52.**

Initials ___________
Date ____________

GENERAL JOURNAL

Date	GL Acct #	Explanation	Post Ref*	Debit	Credit

***Note: Posting reference is "GL and Page Number." For example, GL52.**

Initials __________
Date __________

GENERAL JOURNAL

Date	GL Acct #	Explanation	Post Ref	Debit	Credit

***Note: Posting reference is "GL and Page Number." For example, GL52.**

Initials __________
Date ____________

SALES REGISTER

Date	Customer	Invoice/ Document Number	A/R Acct #	Accounts Receivable 121000	Sales 410000	Inventory 145000	Cost of Goods Sold 510000

Hint: A/R is debited; Sales is credited. Inventory is credited; COGS is debited.

Initials ________
Date ________

CASH RECEIPTS JOURNAL

				Accounts Receivable 121000			Other Account		
Date	Description	Cash 111000	Sales Discount 420000	A/R Acct #	Transaction Amount	Sales 410000	GL Acct #	Transaction Amount	Post Ref*

***Note: Posting reference is "GL and Page Number." For example, GL52.**

Hint: Cash and Sales Discount are debited; A/R and Sales are credited. Other Account is typically credited, although there may also be entries that are debited.

Initials ___________
Date ___________

PURCHASES JOURNAL

				Other Account			Accounts Payable 210000	
Date	Vendor	Vendor Invoice #	Inventory 141000	G/L Acct #	Transaction Amount	Post Ref*	A/P Acct #	Transaction Amount

***Note: Posting reference is "GL and Page Number." For example, GL52.**

Hint: Inventory is debited; Other Account and Accounts Payable are credited.

Initials ____________
Date ____________

CASH DISBURSEMENTS JOURNAL

					Accounts Payable 210000		Other Account		
Date	Check Number	Description	Cash 111000	Inventory 141000	A/P Acct #	Transaction Amount	GL Acct #	Transaction Amount	Post Ref*

***Note: Posting reference is "GL and Page Number." For example, GL52.**

Hint: Cash and Inventory are credited; Accounts Payable is debited. Other Account is typically debited, although there may be entries that are credited.

Initials ___________
Date ___________

PAYROLL JOURNAL[1]

Date	Employee/ SSN	Hours: Regular/ Overtime	Pay: Regular/ Overtime	Gross Pay 601000	FICA Withheld 222200	Medicare Withheld 222300	Federal Income Tax 222100	Net Pay 112000	Check No.

[1] Use two lines for each employee. For example, for an hourly employee, the employee's name, regular hours and regular pay are written on the first line, while the social security number, overtime hours, overtime pay, and all other information are written on the second line.

Hint: Gross Pay is debited; FICA Withheld, Medicare Withheld, Federal Income Tax and Net Pay are credited.

Initials ____________

Date ____________

ACCOUNTS RECEIVABLE SUBSIDIARY LEDGER

0509 | **Alota Wine Distributors**
Pier 32, The Embarcadero
San Francisco, CA 94111
Phone: (415) 975-8566

Terms:
3/15, net 30

Credit Limit:

Date		Description	Debit				Credit				Balance			
12	15	Balance Forward									3	340	283	15

0501 | **Bock Wines and Vines**
Pier 19, The Embarcadero
San Francisco, CA 94111
Phone: (415) 834-9675

Terms:
3/15, net 30

Credit Limit:

Date		Description	Debit				Credit				Balance			
12	15	Balance Forward										39	824	24

0555 | **California Pacific Wine**
Pier 81, The Embarcadero
San Francisco, CA 94111
Phone: (415) 827-8455

Terms:
3/15, net 30

Credit Limit:

Date		Description	Debit				Credit				Balance			
12	15	Balance Forward										47	147	71

0504 | **California Premium Beverage**
39848 South Street
Santa Rosa, CA 95402
Phone: (707) 555-7451
Fax: (707) 555-7452

Terms:
3/15, net 30

Credit Limit:

Date		Description	Debit				Credit				Balance			
12	15	Balance Forward												

Initials ____________
Date ____________

0511	**Diversita Wine and Beer Distributors** 1328 L Street Sacramento, CA 95814 Phone: (916) 441-5517										**Terms:** **3/15, net 30** **Credit Limit:**			
Date		**Description**	**Debit**				**Credit**				**Balance**			
12	15	Balance Forward									1	885	031	06

0505	**Pacific Distribution Co.** 10034 Westborough Boulevard San Francisco, CA 94080 Phone: (415) 555-1532										**Terms:** **3/15, net 30** **Credit Limit:**			
Date		**Description**	**Debit**				**Credit**				**Balance**			
12	15	Balance Forward										39	153	60

0506	**Seaside Distributors, Inc.** 9835 West Hills Road Ukiah, CA 95481 Phone: (707) 555-3102										**Terms:** **3/15, net 30** **Credit Limit:**			
Date		**Description**	**Debit**				**Credit**				**Balance**			
12	15	Balance Forward												

0527	**Ukiah Beer, Wines and Vines** 782 Talmadge Street Ukiah, CA 95482 Phone: (707) 555-8247										**Terms:** **3/15, net 30** **Credit Limit:**			
Date		**Description**	**Debit**				**Credit**				**Balance**			
12	15	Balance Forward										15	231	10

Initials ________
Date ________

PERPETUAL INVENTORY SUBSIDIARY LEDGER

145000 - R130056 Merlot

Date		Description	Trans. Quantity	Cost		Extended Cost			Quantity on Hand	Total Balance		
Dec	15	Balance Forward							83484	385	696	08

145000 - R130061 Cabernet Sauvignon

Date		Description	Trans. Quantity	Cost		Extended Cost			Quantity on Hand	Total Balance		
Dec	15	Balance Forward							65784	276	292	80

145000 - R130064 Cabernet Franc

Date		Description	Trans. Quantity	Cost		Extended Cost			Quantity on Hand	Total Balance		
Dec	15	Balance Forward							5964	26	838	00

Initials ________
Date ________

145000 - R130072 Shiraz

Date		Description	Trans. Quantity	Cost		Extended Cost			Quantity on Hand	Total Balance			
Dec	15	Balance Forward							75888		347	567	04

145000 - W120015 Riesling

Date		Description	Trans. Quantity	Cost		Extended Cost			Quantity on Hand	Total Balance			
Dec	15	Balance Forward							118596		339	184	56

145000 - W120016 Sauvignon Blanc

Date		Description	Trans. Quantity	Cost		Extended Cost			Quantity on Hand	Total Balance			
Dec	15	Balance Forward							93636		267	798	96

Initials __________
Date __________

145000 - W120019 Chenin Blanc

Date		Description	Trans. Quantity	Cost	Extended Cost	Quantity on Hand	Total Balance			
Dec	15	Balance Forward				44532		148	736	88

145000 - W120080 Chardonnay

Date		Description	Trans. Quantity	Cost	Extended Cost	Quantity on Hand	Total Balance			
Dec	15	Balance Forward				420552	1	909	306	08

145000 - S140000 Sparkling Brut

Date		Description	Trans. Quantity	Cost	Extended Cost	Quantity on Hand	Total Balance			
Dec	15	Balance Forward				47064		342	625	91

Initials ________
Date ________

ACCOUNTS PAYABLE SUBSIDIARY LEDGER

D2538 — **Delicio Vineyards**
12701 South Fernwood
Livermore, CA 94550
Phone: (925) 555-1890
Terms: 2/10, net 30

Date		Description	Debit				Credit				Balance			
11	4	Invoice No. 45354						14	563	56		14	563	56

D0999 — **Diversi Vineyards**
8713 Montauk Drive
Napa, CA 94558
(707)515-8575
Terms: 2/10, net 30

Date		Description	Debit				Credit				Balance			
12	15	Balance Forward									2	675	814	93

M0652 — **Mendocino Vineyards**
8654 Witherspoon Way
Hopland, CA 95449
Phone: (707) 555-1890
Terms: 2/10, net 30

Date		Description	Debit				Credit				Balance			
12	15	Balance Forward										28	942	78

M5170 — **Molti Vineyards**
12773 Calma Court
Geyersville, CA 95441
(707)956-8626
Terms: 2/10, net 30

Date		Description	Debit				Credit				Balance			
12	15	Balance Forward									2	268	654	52

Initials ___________
Date ___________

EMPLOYEE PAYROLL SUBSIDIARY LEDGER

Employee Name (Last name, First Name, MI): Bryan, Thomas P.	**Social Security No:** 014-39-4215
Address: 35 Winchester Street	**Phone:** (707) 555-1495
Huntington, CA 95394	
	Date of Birth: 6/14/85
	Date of Employment: 4/25/05
	Date of Termination:

PAY RATE HISTORY

Effective Date	Pay Rate	Pay Type	Position	Filing Status	Withholding Allowances
4/25/XW	15.00	Hourly	Presses	Single	1
4/25/XX	17.50	Hourly	Presses	Single	1

Date: Period Ending	Date: Payroll Date	Hours: Regular	Hours: Overtime	Gross Pay 601000	FICA Withheld 222200	Medicare Withheld 222300	Federal Income Tax 222100	Net Pay
11-30-XX Balance Forward				36 617 81	2 270 30	530 96	4 192 05	29 624 50
12 15	12 15	88 00	4 25	1 651 56	102 40	23 95	188 61	1 336 60

Initials ____________
Date ____________

Employee Name (Last name, First Name, MI): Hissom, Robert T.	**Social Security No:** 349-43-6417
Address: 3187 Heckert Way	**Phone:** (707) 555-1219
Apt. 4A	
Huntington, CA 95394	**Date of Birth:** 11-9-87
	Date of Employment: 1-4-08
	Date of Termination:

PAY RATE HISTORY

Effective Date	Pay Rate	Pay Type	Position	Filing Status	Withholding Allowances			
1-4-XW	14.25	Hourly	Receiving	Single	0			
1-4-XX	15.75	Hourly	Receiving	Single	0			

Date: Period Ending		Date: Payroll Date		Hours: Regular		Hours: Overtime		Gross Pay 601000			FICA Withheld 222200			Medicare Withheld 222300		Federal Income Tax 222100			Net Pay		
11-30-XX Balance Forward								33	642	35	2	085	83	487	81	4	302	76	26	765	95
12	15	12	15	88	00	2	75	1	450	97		89	96	21	04		183	85	1	156	12

Initials ________
Date ________

Employee Name (Last name, First Name, MI): Johnson, Anna C.	**Social Security No:** 296-49-3438
Address: 175 Bunker Hill Lane	**Phone:** (707) 555-3856
Huntington, CA 95394	
	Date of Birth: 9-7-78
	Date of Employment: 2-14-01
	Date of Termination:

PAY RATE HISTORY

Effective Date	Pay Rate	Pay Type	Position	Filing Status	Withholding Allowances
2-14-XW	1,650	Salary	Payroll	Married	3
2-16-XX	1,800	Salary	Acct Sup	Married	3

Date: Period Ending	Date: Payroll Date	Hours: Regular	Hours: Overtime	Gross Pay 601000	FICA Withheld 222200	Medicare Withheld 222300	Federal Income Tax 222100	Net Pay
11-30-XX Balance Forward				39 150 00	2 427 30	567 68	2 157 58	33 997 44
12 15	12 15			1 800 00	111 60	26 10	101 14	1 561 16

Initials ________
Date ________

Employee Name (Last name, First Name, MI): Rodriguez, José G.	**Social Security No:** 124-11-7755
Address: 2953 Whistler Hill Lane	**Phone:** (707) 555-2024
Huntington, CA 95394	
	Date of Birth: 7-7-71
	Date of Employment: 11-3-93
	Date of Termination:

PAY RATE HISTORY

Effective Date	Pay Rate	Pay Type	Position	Filing Status	Withholding Allowances
1-1-XX	3,500	Salary	Supervisor	Married	4

Date: Period Ending	Date: Payroll Date	Hours: Regular	Hours: Overtime	Gross Pay 601000	FICA Withheld 222200	Medicare Withheld 222300	Federal Income Tax 222100	Net Pay
11-30-XX Balance Forward				77 000 00	4 774 00	1 116 50	7 278 04	63 831 46
12 15	12 15			3 500 00	217 00	50 75	330 82	2 901 43

Initials ________
Date ________

FIXED ASSET SUBSIDIARY LEDGER

Asset: Fork Lift

Purchased from: Northern California Equipment

Depreciation Method: SL

Estimated Life: 10 years

Estimated Salvage Value: $ 0

Date			Asset Debit	Asset Credit	Asset Balance	Depreciation Debit	Depreciation Credit	Depreciation Balance	Net Book Value
12	23	XW	18 881 00		18 881 00				18 881 00
12	31	XW					944 05	944 05	17 936 95
1	31	XX					157 34	1 101 39	17 779 61
2	28	XX					157 34	1 258 73	17 622 27
3	31	XX					157 34	1 416 07	17 464 93
4	30	XX					157 34	1 573 41	17 307 59
5	31	XX					157 34	1 730 75	17 150 25
6	30	XX					157 34	1 888 09	16 992 91
7	31	XX					157 34	2 045 43	16 835 57
8	31	XX					157 34	2 202 77	16 678 23
9	30	XX					157 34	2 360 11	16 520 89
10	31	XX					157 34	2 517 45	16 363 55
11	30	XX					157 34	2 674 79	16 206 21
12	31	XX					157 36	2 832 15	16 048 85

Initials ___________
Date ___________

Asset:	**Depreciation Method:**
Purchased from:	**Estimated Life:**
	Estimated Salvage Value:

	Asset			**Depreciation**			
Date	**Debit**	**Credit**	**Balance**	**Debit**	**Credit**	**Balance**	**Net Book Value**

Initials ___________
Date ___________

GENERAL LEDGER

111000 - General Checking Account			Ref	Debit	Credit	Debit Balance
Dec	15	Balance Forward				2 222 927 47

112000 - Payroll Checking Account			Ref	Debit	Credit	Debit Balance
Dec	15	Balance Forward				1 000 00

113000 - Money Market Account			Ref	Debit	Credit	Debit Balance
Dec	15	Balance Forward				782 546 49

114000 - Savings Account			Ref	Debit	Credit	Debit Balance
Dec	15	Balance Forward				51 745 56

119000 - Petty Cash			Ref	Debit	Credit	Debit Balance
Dec	15	Balance Forward				500 00

121000 - Accounts Receivable			Ref	Debit	Credit	Debit Balance
Dec	15	Balance Forward				5 366 670 86

*Note: Use the Reference column to refer to the applicable journal. For example, use SR and the page number (e.g., SR29) to refer to the appropriate page of the sales register. Similarly, use CD and the page number to refer to the appropriate page of the cash disbursements journal.

Initials ________
Date ________

129000 – Allowance for Bad Debts			Ref	Debit				Credit				Credit Balance			
Dec	15	Balance Forward											95	401	58

141000 – Inventory -- Production			Ref	Debit				Credit				Debit Balance			
Dec	15	Balance Forward										11	564	851	56

145000 - Inventory – Finished Goods			Ref	Debit				Credit				Debit Balance			
Dec	15	Balance Forward										4	044	046	31

150000 - Prepaid Expenses			Ref	Debit				Credit				Debit Balance			
Dec	15	Balance Forward											142	465	96

160000 - Land and Buildings			Ref	Debit				Credit				Debit Balance			
Dec	15	Balance Forward										16	358	487	34

170000 - Equipment			Ref	Debit				Credit				Debit Balance			
Dec	15	Balance Forward										13	844	881	10

Initials __________
Date __________

180000 - Accumulated Depreciation			Ref	Debit				Credit				Credit Balance			
Dec	15	Balance Forward										15	233	662	97

191000 - Investments			Ref	Debit				Credit				Debit Balance			
Dec	15	Balance Forward										3	070	227	56

210000 - Accounts Payable			Ref	Debit				Credit				Credit Balance			
Dec	15	Balance Forward										4	987	975	79

222100 - Federal Income Tax Withheld			Ref	Debit				Credit				Credit Balance			
Dec	15	Balance Forward											66	739	08

222200 - FICA Withheld			Ref	Debit				Credit				Credit Balance			
Dec	15	Balance Forward											12	237	64

222300 - Medicare Withheld			Ref	Debit				Credit				Credit Balance			
Dec	15	Balance Forward											2	862	01

Initials ________
Date ________

223100 - FICA Payable – Employer			**Ref**	**Debit**	**Credit**	**Credit Balance**		
Dec	15	Balance Forward				12	237	64

223200 - Medicare Payable – Employer			**Ref**	**Debit**	**Credit**	**Credit Balance**		
Dec	15	Balance Forward				2	862	01

223300 - Unemployment Taxes Payable			**Ref**	**Debit**	**Credit**	**Credit Balance**		
Dec	15	Balance Forward					943	57

230000 – Other Accrued Expenses			**Ref**	**Debit**	**Credit**	**Credit Balance**		
Dec	15	Balance Forward				599	348	98

235000 - Federal Income Taxes Payable			**Ref**	**Debit**	**Credit**	**Credit Balance**		
Dec	15	Balance Forward					0	00

239000 - Dividends Payable			**Ref**	**Debit**	**Credit**	**Credit Balance**		
Dec	15	Balance Forward					0	00

Initials __________
Date __________

240000 - Mortgages Payable			Ref	Debit	Credit	Credit Balance
Dec	15	Balance Forward				7 639 067 73

261000 - Notes Payable			Ref	Debit	Credit	Credit Balance
Dec	15	Balance Forward				841 000 00

310000 - Common Stock			Ref	Debit	Credit	Credit Balance
Dec	15	Balance Forward				90 000 00

311000 - PIC in Excess of Par - Common			Ref	Debit	Credit	Credit Balance
Dec	15	Balance Forward				3 567 265 00

312000 - Dividends - Common			Ref	Debit	Credit	Debit Balance
Dec	15	Balance Forward				0 00

390000 - Retained Earnings			Ref	Debit	Credit	Credit Balance
Dec	15	Balance Forward				22 064 134 78

Initials ___________
Date ___________

410000 - Sales			Ref	Debit	Credit	Credit Balance
Dec	15	Balance Forward				22 264 431 15

420000 - Sales Discounts			Ref	Debit	Credit	Debit Balance
Dec	15	Balance Forward				346 741 36

430000 - Sales Returns and Allowances			Ref	Debit	Credit	Debit Balance
Dec	15	Balance Forward				15 588 47

451000 - Gain/Loss – Fixed Assets			Ref	Debit	Credit	Credit Balance
Dec	15	Balance Forward				0 00

452000 - Gain/Loss – Marketable Securities			Ref	Debit	Credit	Credit Balance
Dec	15	Balance Forward				0 00

491000 - Dividend Income			Ref	Debit	Credit	Credit Balance
Dec	15	Balance Forward				4 000 00

Initials ________
Date ________

492000 - Interest Income			Ref	Debit	Credit	Credit Balance
Dec	15	Balance Forward				23 482 56

510000 - Cost of Goods Sold			Ref	Debit	Credit	Debit Balance
Dec	15	Balance Forward				11 514 092 11

601000 - Wages and Salaries Expense			Ref	Debit	Credit	Debit Balance
Dec	15	Balance Forward				1 965 164 11

601500 - Sales Commission Expense			Ref	Debit	Credit	Debit Balance
Dec	15	Balance Forward				771 665 60

602100 - FICA Tax Expense			Ref	Debit	Credit	Debit Balance
Dec	15	Balance Forward				244 124 52

602200 - Medicare Tax Expense			Ref	Debit	Credit	Debit Balance
Dec	15	Balance Forward				57 093 62

Initials __________
Date __________

602300 - FUTA Expense			**Ref**	**Debit**			**Credit**			**Debit Balance**		
Dec	15	Balance Forward									7	392	00

602400 - SUTA Expense			**Ref**	**Debit**			**Credit**			**Debit Balance**		
Dec	15	Balance Forward								22	176	00

611000 - Utilities Expense			**Ref**	**Debit**			**Credit**			**Debit Balance**		
Dec	15	Balance Forward								307	067	05

611300 - Irrigation & Waste Disp. Expense			**Ref**	**Debit**			**Credit**			**Debit Balance**		
Dec	15	Balance Forward								230	910	91

612000 - Landscaping Expense			**Ref**	**Debit**			**Credit**			**Debit Balance**		
Dec	15	Balance Forward								142	475	69

621000 - Advertising Expense			**Ref**	**Debit**			**Credit**			**Debit Balance**		
Dec	15	Balance Forward								296	794	33

Initials ____________
Date ____________

623000 - Marketing Expense			Ref	Debit	Credit	Debit Balance		
Dec	15	Balance Forward				192	865	67

624000 - Festivals & Competitions Expense			Ref	Debit	Credit	Debit Balance		
Dec	15	Balance Forward				238	654	75

631000 - Telephone Expense			Ref	Debit	Credit	Debit Balance		
Dec	15	Balance Forward				37	584	73

632000 - Internet & Computer Expense			Ref	Debit	Credit	Debit Balance		
Dec	15	Balance Forward				14	475	00

633000 - Postage Expense			Ref	Debit	Credit	Debit Balance		
Dec	15	Balance Forward				35	117	66

641000 - Legal & Accounting Fees			Ref	Debit	Credit	Debit Balance		
Dec	15	Balance Forward				88	425	50

Initials ___________
Date ___________

643000 - Other Consulting Fees			Ref	Debit			Credit			Debit Balance		
Dec	15	Balance Forward								12	500	00

651000 - Office Supplies Expense			Ref	Debit			Credit			Debit Balance		
Dec	15	Balance Forward								58	689	68

660000 - Data Processing Expense			Ref	Debit			Credit			Debit Balance		
Dec	15	Balance Forward								9	743	89

670000 - Depreciation Expense			Ref	Debit			Credit			Debit Balance			
Dec	15	Balance Forward								1	092	832	66

680000 - Travel and Entertainment Expense			Ref	Debit			Credit			Debit Balance		
Dec	15	Balance Forward								169	405	86

691000 – Other Insurance Expense			Ref	Debit			Credit			Debit Balance		
Dec	15	Balance Forward								115	058	55

Initials __________
Date ___________

692000 – Medical Insurance			Ref	Debit	Credit	Debit Balance		
Dec	15	Balance Forward				192	154	80

693000 - Workmen's Compensation Insurance			Ref	Debit	Credit	Debit Balance		
Dec	15	Balance Forward				139	750	00

699000 - Other Employee Benefits Expense			Ref	Debit	Credit	Debit Balance		
Dec	15	Balance Forward				175	643	90

700000 - Dues and Subscriptions Expense			Ref	Debit	Credit	Debit Balance		
Dec	15	Balance Forward				32	076	00

711000 - Federal Income Tax Expense			Ref	Debit	Credit	Debit Balance		
Dec	15	Balance Forward				857	595	76

712000 - Property Tax Expense			Ref	Debit	Credit	Debit Balance		
Dec	15	Balance Forward				19	875	00

Initials ____________
Date ____________

721000 - Repairs and Maintenance Expense			Ref	Debit			Credit			Debit Balance		
Dec	15	Balance Forward								71	974	93

731000 - Automobile Expense			Ref	Debit			Credit			Debit Balance		
Dec	15	Balance Forward								81	493	45

740000 - Lease Expense			Ref	Debit			Credit			Debit Balance		
Dec	15	Balance Forward								113	607	56

791000 - Bad Debt Expense			Ref	Debit			Credit			Debit Balance		
Dec	15	Balance Forward									0	00

792000 - Miscellaneous Expense			Ref	Debit			Credit			Debit Balance		
Dec	15	Balance Forward								26	575	63

793000 - Interest Expense			Ref	Debit			Credit			Debit Balance		
Dec	15	Balance Forward								359	915	53

Initials ________
Date ________

TRANSACTION SET B

The books have been posted through December 15, 20XX. The following selected transactions have been extracted from the period December 16 through December 31, 20XX and are to be completed in accordance with the policies and procedures explained above. Documents to be completed can be found in the Document Packet. For all required signatures on these documents sign your name. Supporting documentation for many of the transactions is provided behind the Year-End Procedures on page 12, followed by all necessary journals and ledgers. Additional documentation is found behind the Transaction Set B.

Note that the current year transactions are denoted as 20XX; prior year transactions are denoted as 20XW; transactions for the subsequent year are denoted as 20XY. Your instructor will provide you with the appropriate current year and you can make the fill in the dates accordingly for all transactions.

December	Transaction
16	Receive a purchase order from California Premium Beverage (page 63). Fill and ship the order. Complete Invoice No. 15535, Bill of Lading No. 136480 and record the sale in the journals and ledgers. W. A. Bierkstahler is the sales account representative. Relevant data: shipment weight - 12,532 lbs., trailer # - 122302, serial # - 999356278. The carrier is CA Express. Leave the CID No. blank.
16	Order 31 tons white grapes at $1,925.11 per ton from Mendocino Vineyards. The item number for the white grapes is WG1003. Complete Purchase Order No. 9682. Relevant data: date required - Dec. 22, shipper - Longhorn Shippers, Inc., buyer - Franz Bieler, supplier # - M0652.
16	Purchase a 20XX Ford truck for $31,250.00. The terms include a $6,250.00 down payment and a 3-year, 6% promissory note to Ford Credit for the remaining $25,000.00. Principal and interest on the note are due monthly beginning January 4, 20XY. The company expects the truck to have a useful life of 5 years and no salvage value. Prepare Check No. 19257 payable to Potter Valley Ford for the down payment and record the transaction in the journals and ledgers.
16	The Board of Directors of Chateau Americana authorized a $60,000 cash dividend payable on December 31st to the stockholders of record on December 26th. Use Check No. 19476 when paid.
17	Receive a phone complaint from Seaside Distributors about a case of Chenin Blanc that was damaged in shipment. The case was part of Invoice No. 15175, dated November 5, 20XX, in the amount of $20,438.40. Seaside paid the invoice on November 19, 20XX and took advantage of the discount (terms 3/15, net 30). Prepare Credit Memo No. 2753 to write-off the damaged inventory that was not returned, and prepare Check No. 19286 to reimburse Seaside for the damaged goods. Record the transactions in the journals and ledgers. W. A. Bierkstahler is the sales account representative. Relevant data: customer PO # - MZ5713. (Note: Be sure to review ***Returns and Allowances*** on Page 6.)

December	Transaction
19	Receive notification of $850 interest income that was deposited directly into the checking account from a certificate of deposit from State Employees' Credit Union. Record the cash receipt in the journals and ledgers.
19	Receive payment in full from Pacific Distribution Co. on Invoice No. 15243 dated November 13, 20XX, in the amount of $19,576.80 (page 19). Enter the receipt on Cash Receipts Summary No. 5712 and record the cash receipt in the journals and ledgers.
19	Receive a purchase order (page 64) with payment (page 65) from Sonoma Distributors. Fill and ship the order. Complete Invoice No. C2489, enter the receipt on Cash Receipts Summary No. 5712, and record the sale in the journals and ledgers. W. A. Bierkstahler is the sales account representative. Relevant data: shipment weight - 7,650 lbs., trailer # - 279AJ1, serial # - 919515094. (Hint: Use the Other Account column to post Inventory and Cost of Goods Sold.) **DO NOT** create a Bill of Lading for this purchase order.
22	Receive 18 tons red grapes at $2,437.40 per ton from Mendocino Vineyards. Also received Invoice No. M7634 from Mendocino Vineyards with the shipment (page 68). Terms on the invoice are 2/10, net 30. Complete Receiving Report No. 17251 and record the inventory in the journals and ledgers using the gross method.
26	Receive utility bill from Pacific Gas and Electric in the amount of $18,887.62 (page 23). Prepare Check No. 19402 and record the payment in the journals and ledgers.
30	Receive Brokerage Advice from Edwards Jones for purchase of 500 shares of Microsoft at $74.26 per share plus $400 broker's commission (page 24). Prepare Check No. 19468 and record the purchase in the journals and ledgers.
31	Receive payment in full for the December 16 purchase from California Premium Beverage (page 66). Enter the cash receipt on Cash Receipts Summary No. 5718 and record the cash receipt in the journals and ledgers.
31	Prepare Check No. 19473 payable to Mendocino Vineyards for the shipment received on December 22 and record the payment in the journals and ledgers.
31	Prepare Payroll Checks (Nos. 7111-7114) for Anna Johnson, José Rodriguez, Tom Bryan, and Bob Hissom. Time cards for Tom and Bob are on pages 26-27. Prepare Check No. 19474 to transfer cash from the general cash account to the payroll account. Record the payroll transactions in the journals and ledgers.
31	Prepare Check No. 19475 to repay $75,000 of the principal on long-term debt to Bank of Huntington and record the payment in the journals and ledgers.

Refer to Pages 12-13 for **Month-End** and **Year-End Procedures**.

The Winery at Chateau Americana
Price List

Inventory Code	Description	Standard Cost (per bottle)	Selling Price (per bottle)
R130064	Cabernet Franc	$ 5.74	$ 11.48
R130061	Cabernet Sauvignon	5.23	9.94
R130056	Merlot	5.17	10.08
R130072	Shiraz	5.36	11.71
W120080	Chardonnay	10.07	13.83
W120019	Chenin Blanc	5.03	9.51
W120015	Riesling	5.94	10.54
W120016	Sauvignon Blanc	6.01	11.27
S140000	Sparkling Brut	10.76	16.36

PURCHASE ORDER

California Premium Beverage

39848 South Street
Santa Rosa, CA 95402
Phone (707) 555-7451 Fax (707) 555-7452

To:
Chateau Americana
3003 Vineyard Way
Huntington, CA 95394

Ship To:
California Premium Beverage
39848 South Street
Santa Rosa, CA 95402

ABC Permit #: A59782

P.O. DATE	P.O. NUMBER	SHIPPED VIA	F.O.B. POINT	TERMS
12/13/XX	8746	CA Express	Destination	3/15, net 30

ITEM NO	QTY	SIZE	DESCRIPTION	UNIT PRICE	TOTAL
W120015	1512	0.750	Riesling	10.54	15,936.48
W120016	504	0.750	Sauvignon Blanc	11.27	5,680.08
W120019	336	0.750	Chenin Blanc	9.51	3,195.36
R130061	1176	0.750	Cabernet Sauvignon	9.94	11,689.44
R130056	672	0.750	Merlot	10.08	6,773.76
S140000	240	0.750	Sparkling Brut	16.36	3,926.40
W120080	336	0.750	Chardonnay	13.83	4,646.88
				TOTAL	51,848.40

Jorge Gonzalez — Authorized by
12/13/XX — Date

PURCHASE ORDER

PO Number: 4376
Date: 12/19/XX

To:
Chateau Americana
3003 Vineyard Way
Huntington, CA 95394

Ship To:
SONOMA DISTRIBUTORS
3224 Greenlawn Street
Ukiah, CA 95482
Phone (707) 555-1705 Fax (707) 555-1706

SHIPPED VIA	ABC #	F.O.B. POINT	TERMS
United Express	A557912	Huntington	Cash

ITEM NO	QTY	SIZE	DESCRIPTION	UNIT PRICE	TOTAL
W120015	480	0.750	Riesling	10.54	5,059.20
W120080	468	0.750	Chardonnay	13.83	6,472.44
W120019	300	0.750	Chenin Blanc	9.51	2,853.00
R130072	780	0.750	Shiraz	11.71	9,133.80
R130056	672	0.750	Merlot	10.08	6,773.76
				TOTAL	30,292.20

Chrystal Harrington — 12/19/XX
Authorized by — Date

Sonoma Distributors
3224 Greenlawn Street
Ukiah, CA 95482

Humboldt Bank
Ukiah, CA 95482

17003

Date 12/19/XX

PAY Thirty Thousand Two Hundred Ninety-Two and 20/100 Dollars ---------------- $ 30,292.20

To the order of
Chateau Americana
3003 Vineyard Way
Huntington, CA 95394

- SAMPLE, DO NOT CASH -

⑆000000⑆ ⑈000000000⑈ 17003

Sonoma Distributors **17003**

Reference	Discount	Net Amount
Payment for PO 4376		$30,292.20

California Premium Beverage | Bay View Bank | **21803**

39848 South Street
Santa Rosa, CA 95402

Bay View Bank
Santa Rosa, CA 95407

Date 12/29/XX

PAY Fifty Thousand Two Hundred Ninety-Two and 95/100 Dollars ----------------- $ 50,292.95

To The Order Of

Chateau Americana
3003 Vineyard Way
Huntington, CA 95394

- SAMPLE, DO NOT CASH -

¦:000000¦: :000000000: 21803

California Premium Beverage **21803**

Reference	Discount	Net Amount
# 0504 Invoice 15535	1,555.45	$50,292.95

CUSTOMER INVOICE

Invoice Number **M7634**

Mendocino Vineyards
8654 Witherspoon Way
Hopland, CA 95449
Phone: (707) 555-1890

Invoice Date 12/20/20XX

Sold To:
Chateau Americana, Inc.
3003 Vineyard Way
Huntington, CA 95394

Ship To:
Chateau Americana, Inc.
3003 Vineyard Way
Huntington, CA 95394

Credit Terms: 2/10, Net 30

Customer I.D	Customer P.O. Number
CHATAM	9660

Description	Product Number	Quantity	Cost	Extended
Cabernet Sauvignon Grapes	CS1250	18 tons	$2,437.40	$43,873.20

Total Cost: $43,873.20

Comments:

Distribution: Copy 1 — Accounting; Copy 2 – Shipping; Copy 3 – Customer

TRANSACTION SET C

The books have been posted through December 15, 20XX. The following selected transactions have been extracted from the period December 16 through December 31, 20XX and are to be completed in accordance with the policies and procedures explained above. Documents to be completed can be found in the Document Packet. For all required signatures on these documents sign your name. Supporting documentation for many of the transactions is provided behind the Year-End Procedures on page 12, followed by all necessary journals and ledgers. Additional documentation is found behind the Transaction Set C.

Note that the current year transactions are denoted as 20XX; prior year transactions are denoted as 20XW; transactions for the subsequent year are denoted as 20XY. Your instructor will provide you with the appropriate current year and you can make the fill in the dates accordingly for all transactions.

December	Transaction
16	Receive a purchase order from California Premium Beverage (page 72). Fill and ship the order. Complete Invoice No. 15535, Bill of Lading No. 136480 and record the sale in the journals and ledgers. W. A. Bierkstahler is the sales account representative. Relevant data: shipment weight - 12,532 lbs., trailer # - 122302, serial # - 999356278. The carrier is CA Express. Leave the CID No. blank.
16	Order 31 tons white grapes at $1,936.78 per ton from Mendocino Vineyards. The item number for the white grapes is WG1003. Complete Purchase Order No. 9682. Relevant data: date required – January 15, 20XY, shipper - Longhorn Shippers, Inc., buyer - Franz Bieler, supplier # - M0652.
16	Purchase a 2004 Ford truck for $36,750.00. The terms include a $5,250.00 down payment and a 3-year, 6% promissory note to Ford Credit for the remaining $31,500.00. Principal and interest on the note are due monthly beginning January 4, 20XY. The company expects the truck to have a useful life of 5 years and no salvage value. Prepare Check No. 19257 payable to Potter Valley Ford for the down payment and record the transaction in the journals and ledgers.
16	Sell Fork Lift that was purchased on December 23, 20XW for $19,250.00 to Castle Vineyards. Record the transactions in the journals and ledgers (the Fork Lift depreciation for December was calculated before the sale took place and depreciation for the year needs to be adjusted). Enter receipt on Cash Receipts Summary No. 5712.
17	Receive a phone complaint from Seaside Distributors about a case of Chenin Blanc that was damaged in shipment. The case was part of Invoice No. 15175, dated November 5, 20XX, in the amount of $20,438.40. Seaside paid the invoice on November 19, 20XX and took advantage of the discount (terms 3/15, net 30). Prepare Credit Memo No. 2753 to write-off the damaged inventory that was not returned, and prepare Check No. 19286 to reimburse Seaside for the damaged goods. Record the transactions in the journals and ledgers. W.A. Bierkstahler is the sales account representative. Relevant data: customer PO # - MZ5713. (Note: Be sure to review ***Returns and Allowances*** on Page 6.)

December	Transaction
19	Receive notification of $850 interest income that was deposited directly into the checking account from a certificate of deposit from State Employees' Credit Union. Record the cash receipt in the journals and ledgers.
19	Receive payment in full from Pacific Distribution Co. on Invoice No. 15243 dated November 13, 20XX, in the amount of $20,164.30 (page 19). Enter the receipt on Cash Receipts Summary No. 5712 and record the cash receipt in the journals and ledgers.
19	Receive a purchase order (page 73) with payment (page 74) from Sonoma Distributors. Fill and ship the order. Complete Invoice No. C2489, enter the receipt on Cash Receipts Summary No. 5712, and record the sale in the journals and ledgers. W. A. Bierkstahler is the sales account representative. Relevant data: shipment weight - 7,650 lbs., trailer # - 279AJ1, serial # - 919515094. (Hint: Use the Other Account column to post Inventory and Cost of Goods Sold.) **DO NOT** create a Bill of Lading for this purchase order.
22	Receive 23 tons red grapes at $2,489.21 per ton from Mendocino Vineyards. Also received Invoice No. M7634 from Mendocino Vineyards with the shipment (page 75). Terms on the invoice are 2/10, net 30. Complete Receiving Report No. 17251 and record the inventory in the journals and ledgers using the gross method.
26	Receive utility bill from Pacific Gas and Electric in the amount of $19,271.12 (page 76). Prepare Check No. 19402 and record the payment in the journals and ledgers.
30	Receive Brokerage Advice from Edwards Jones for purchase of 500 shares of Microsoft at $74.26 per share plus $400 broker's commission (page 24). Prepare Check No. 19468 and record the purchase in the journals and ledgers.
31	Receive payment in full for the December 16 purchase from California Premium Beverage (page 77). Enter the cash receipt on Cash Receipts Summary No. 5718 and record the cash receipt in the journals and ledgers.
31	Prepare Check No. 19473 payable to Mendocino Vineyards for the shipment received on December 22 and record the payment in the journals and ledgers.
31	Prepare Payroll Checks (Nos. 7111-7114) for Anna Johnson, José Rodriguez, Tom Bryan, and Bob Hissom. Time cards for Tom and Bob are on pages 26-27. Prepare Check No. 19474 to transfer cash from the general cash account to the payroll account. Record the payroll transactions in the journals and ledgers.
31	Prepare Check No. 19475 to repay $90,000 of the principal on long-term debt to Bank of Huntington and record the payment in the journals and ledgers.

Refer to Pages 12-13 for **Month-End** and **Year-End Procedures**.

The Winery at Chateau Americana
Price List

Inventory Code	Description	Standard Cost (per bottle)	Selling Price (per bottle)
R130064	Cabernet Franc	$ 7.25	$ 13.76
R130061	Cabernet Sauvignon	6.49	12.33
R130056	Merlot	6.98	13.26
R130072	Shiraz	7.17	13.63
W120080	Chardonnay	10.57	18.50
W120019	Chenin Blanc	6.23	10.90
W120015	Riesling	6.08	10.64
W120016	Sauvignon Blanc	9.04	15.82
S140000	Sparkling Brut	11.25	21.94

PURCHASE ORDER

California Premium Beverage

39848 South Street
Santa Rosa, CA 95402
Phone (707) 555-7451 Fax (707) 555-7452

To:
Chateau Americana
3003 Vineyard Way
Huntington, CA 95394

Ship To:
California Premium Beverage
39848 South Street
Santa Rosa, CA 95402

ABC Permit #: A59782

P.O. DATE	P.O. NUMBER	SHIPPED VIA	F.O.B. POINT	TERMS
12/13/XX	8746	CA Express	Destination	3/15, net 30

ITEM NO	QTY	SIZE	DESCRIPTION	UNIT PRICE	TOTAL
W120015	1512	0.750	Riesling	10.64	16,087.68
W120016	504	0.750	Sauvignon Blanc	15.82	7,973.28
W120019	336	0.750	Chenin Blanc	10.90	3,662.40
R130061	1176	0.750	Cabernet Sauvignon	12.33	14,500.08
R130056	672	0.750	Merlot	13.26	8,910.72
S140000	240	0.750	Sparkling Brut	21.94	5,265.60
W120080	336	0.750	Chardonnay	18.50	6,216.00
				TOTAL	62,615.76

Jorge Gonzalez — Authorized by

12/13/XX — Date

PURCHASE ORDER

PO Number: 4376
Date: 12/19/XX

To:
Chateau Americana
3003 Vineyard Way
Huntington, CA 95394

Ship To:
SONOMA DISTRIBUTORS
3224 Greenlawn Street
Ukiah, CA 95482
Phone (707) 555-1705 Fax (707) 555-1706

SHIPPED VIA	ABC #	F.O.B. POINT	TERMS
United Express	A557912	Huntington	Cash

ITEM NO	QTY	SIZE	DESCRIPTION	UNIT PRICE	TOTAL
W120015	480	0.750	Riesling	10.64	5,107.20
W120080	468	0.750	Chardonnay	18.50	8,658.00
W120019	300	0.750	Chenin Blanc	10.90	3,270.00
R130072	780	0.750	Shiraz	13.63	10,631.40
R130056	672	0.750	Merlot	13.26	8,910.72
				TOTAL	36,577.32

Chrystal Harrington — 12/19/XX
Authorized by — Date

Sonoma Distributors
3224 Greenlawn Street
Ukiah, CA 95482

Humboldt Bank
Ukiah, CA 95482

17003

Date 12/19/XX

PAY Thirty-six Thousand Five Hundred Seventy-seven and 32/100 Dollars -------------- $ 36,577.32

To the order of Chateau Americana
3003 Vineyard Way
Huntington, CA 95394

- SAMPLE, DO NOT CASH -

⑆000000⑆ ⑈000000000⑈ 17003

Sonoma Distributors **17003**

Reference	Discount	Net Amount
Payment for PO 4376		$36,577.32

CUSTOMER INVOICE

Invoice Number **M7634**

Invoice Date 12/20/20XX

Mendocino Vineyards
8654 Witherspoon Way
Hopland, CA 95449
Phone: (707) 555-1890

Sold To:
Chateau Americana, Inc.
3003 Vineyard Way
Huntington, CA 95394

Credit Terms: 2/10, Net 30

Ship To:
Chateau Americana, Inc.
3003 Vineyard Way
Huntington, CA 95394

Customer I.D	Customer P.O. Number
CHATAM	9660

Description	Product Number	Quantity	Cost	Extended
Cabernet Sauvignon Grapes	CS1250	23 tons	$2,489.21	$57,251.83

Total Cost: $57,251.83

Comments:

Distribution: Copy 1 — Accounting; Copy 2 – Shipping; Copy 3 – Customer

Payment Coupon

Bill Date: 12/23/20XX

Please Pay by 01/17/20XX
$19,271.12

Amount Enclosed

Account No. 21790-1879

Chateau Americana, Inc.
3003 Vineyard Way
Huntington, CA 95394

Send Payment to:

Pacific Gas and Electric
P.O. Box 2575
San Francisco, CA 94103

Retain bottom portion for your records, detach and return stub with payment.

Service	Chateau Americana, Inc.	Your Account Number	Rate Class	Billing Date
For:	3003 Vineyard Way Huntington, CA 95394	**21790-1879**	**Commercial**	**12/23/20XX**

Meter Number	Service Period	Days	Type of Reading	Multiplier	Units	Meter Readings Current	Meter Readings Past	Usage
68869800	**11/23/XX – 12/23/XX**	**31**	**Actual**	**1**	**KWH**	**1098412**	**1001301**	**97111**
Previous Balance								16,895.53
Payment								16,895.53
Balance Forward								0.00
Current Charges								19,271.12
							Due Date	**Total Due**
							01/17/20XX	19,271.12

Pacific Gas and Electric
1000 Energy Drive, San Francisco, CA 94103, (415) 973-8943

California Premium Beverage **21803**
39848 South Street
Santa Rosa, CA 95402

Bay View Bank
Santa Rosa, CA 95407

Date 12/29/XX

PAY Sixty Thousand Seven Hundred Thirty-seven and 29/100 Dollars ------------------ $ 60,737.29

To The Order Of
Chateau Americana
3003 Vineyard Way
Huntington, CA 95394

- SAMPLE, DO NOT CASH -

⑆000000⑆ ⑈000000000⑈ 21803

California Premium Beverage **21803**

Reference	Discount	Net Amount
# 0504 Invoice 15535	1,878.47	$60,737.29